PIANO
Adventures® *by Nancy and Randall Faber*
THE BASIC PIANO METHOD

CONTENTS

An alphabetical listing of p   *er.*

T0079410

Review Test

Rhythm

1. Fill in the blanks below.

In **4/4** ♩♩♩♩ = ____ beat(s)   In **3/4** 𝅘𝅥𝅮𝅘𝅥𝅮𝅘𝅥𝅮³ = ____ beat(s)

In **3/8** ♩. = ____ beat(s)   In **6/8** ♩ = ____ beat(s)

2. Draw bar lines for the following time signatures.

Write **1 2 3 4** under the correct beats.

Write **1 2 3 4 5 6** under the correct beats.

Extra Credit: Can you play each rhythm on the piano? Use any note of your choice.

Reading

3. Write the correct interval in the blank: 2nd, 3rd, 4th, 5th, 6th, 7th, 8ve (octave)

Then play the example.

Clementi

4. Name the major and relative minor key for each key signature below.

—— major   —— major   —— major
    or   or   or
—— minor   —— minor   —— minor

FF109

Theory

5. Add the correct sharps or flats to complete each scale.

A major scale

E major scale

D natural minor scale

A harmonic minor scale

6. Complete the sharp pattern (7 sharps) in both clefs.

7. Write a 4-note V7 chord in **root position** in these keys:

F major

V7

G major

V7

Symbols & Terms

8. Match each symbol or term to the correct description with a connecting line.

sequence

adagio

poco a poco

sfz

molto

harmonic minor scale

root position

1st inversion

2nd inversion

- the 5th of the chord is the lowest note
- little by little
- very
- slow
- grace note
- natural minor scale with a raised 7th
- a musical pattern repeated on a different pitch
- a sudden, strong accent
- the root (chord name) is the lowest note
- the 3rd of the chord is the lowest note

Review Piece

Sevenths are commonly used in jazz. Practice left-hand 7ths with this jazz warm-up.

Jazz Warm-up

Jazz Reflection

N. Faber

Freely, with expression (♩ = 100-108)

FF109

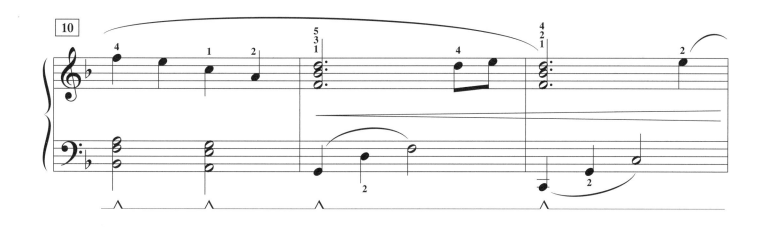

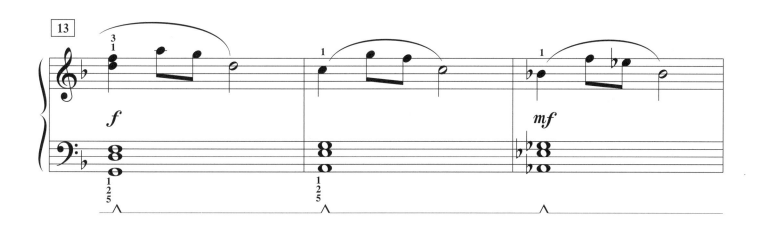

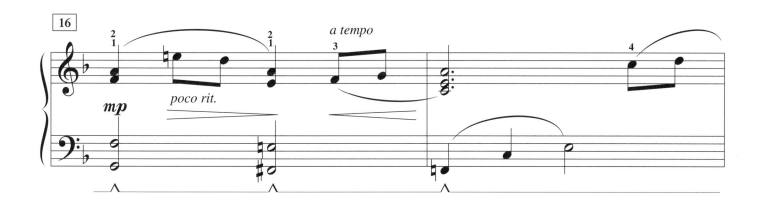

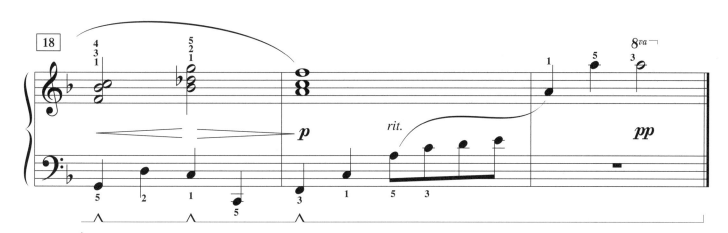

DISCOVERY

Point out a pattern and sequence in this piece.

A **triad** is a 3-note chord built in 3rds.

All major and minor chords and their inversions are triads.

Play these **I, IV,** and **V** triads, naming them aloud: **tonic, subdominant,** and **dominant.**

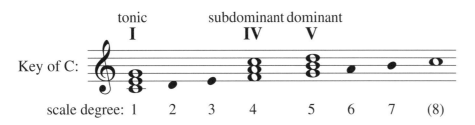

Key of C:

tonic **I**   subdominant **IV**   dominant **V**

scale degree: 1   2   3   4   5   6   7   (8)

Coral Reef Etude

(Inversion Study in C)

Flowing (♩. = 76-88)

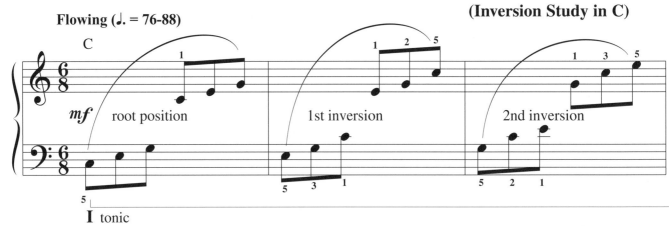

mf   root position   1st inversion   2nd inversion

I tonic

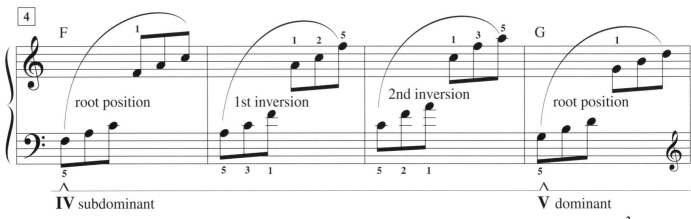

root position   1st inversion   2nd inversion   root position

IV subdominant   **V** dominant

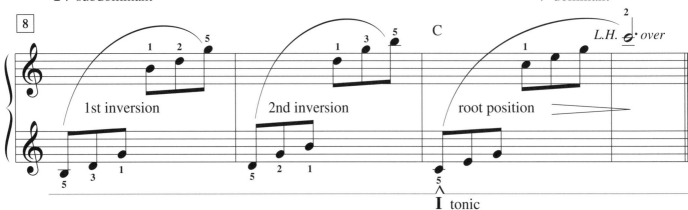

1st inversion   2nd inversion   root position

L.H. over

I tonic

DISCOVERY

Transpose *Coral Reef Etude* to the Key of G major.

In the Key of G: the tonic is _____, the subdominant is _____, the dominant is _____.

Cadences

A *cadence* is a progression of chords that leads to a natural resting point in the music.
A cadence occurs at the end of a phrase, section, or piece.
Cadences usually end on a **I** or **V** chord.

Play these cadences. *Listen* for the natural resting point in the music.

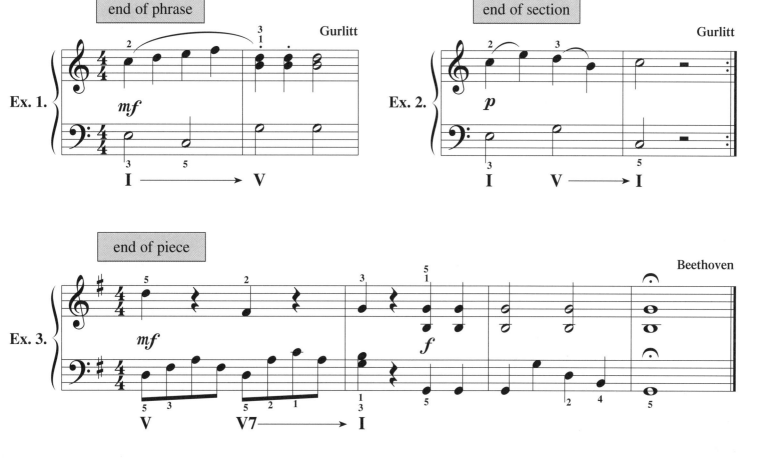

"Grand Cadence"

Practice and memorize this cadence.
Your teacher may ask to transpose to other keys.

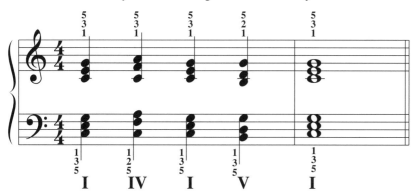

Transposition Record	
Key of G major	❑
Key of D major	❑
Key of A major	❑
Key of E major	❑
Key of F major	❑

CREATIVE Can you make up a **broken chord exercise** using the chords of the "Grand Cadence"?

Practice Techniques for the Advancing Pianist

1. Practice hands separately for correct **notes and rhythm**.

2. Play hands together S-L-O-W-L-Y for **articulation**.
   (staccato and legato touches)   ♪ = 100-108

3. Play at a moderate tempo hands together, focusing on **dynamics**.
   Mark any difficult measures with an X and give them extra practice.

Sonatina
Op. 36, No. 1
(3rd movement)

Muzio Clementi
(1752-1832, Italy)
original form

cadence on
I or **V**? *(circle one)*

Vivace (pronounced "vee-VAH-chay") - means quick and lively

FF1093

Performance p. 4   Theory p. 4

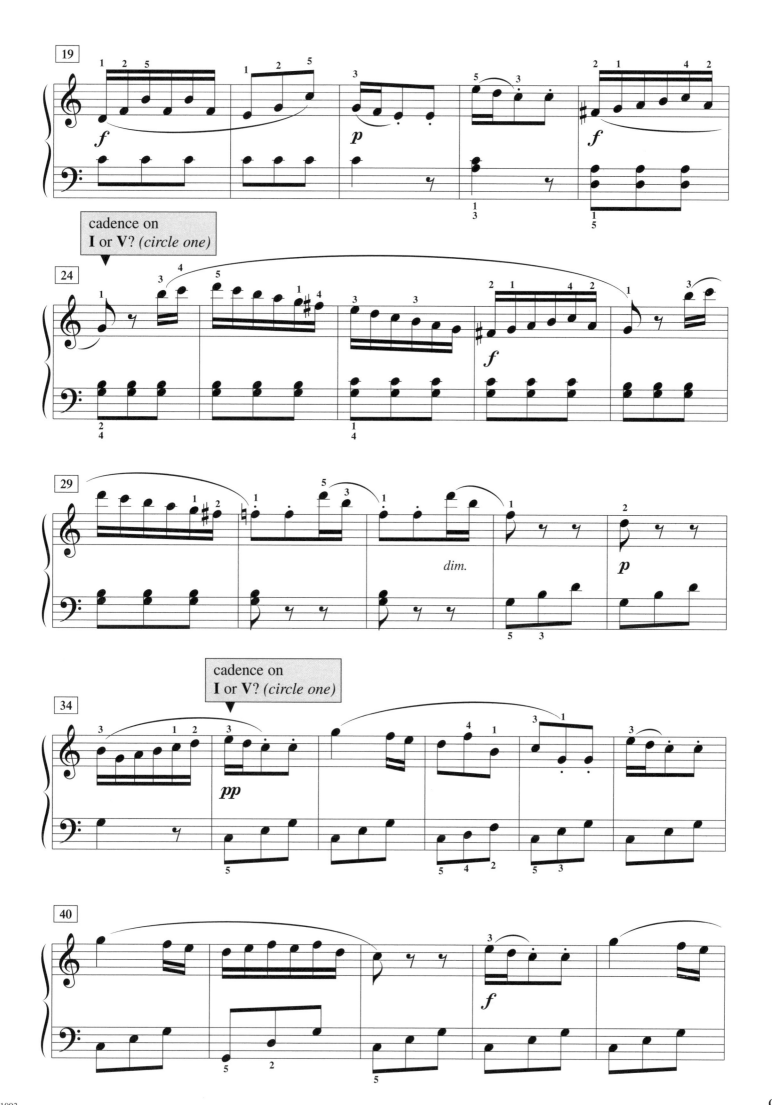

cadence on
I or **V**? *(circle one)*

DISCOVERY How many times is the opening 8-measure theme stated?
three times   four times   five times   *(circle one)*

FF109

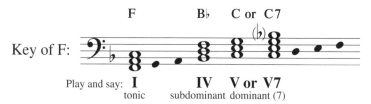

Key of F:

Play and say: **I**   **IV**   **V or V7**
       tonic   subdominant   dominant (7)

Blue Etude

(Inversion Study in F)

Moderately (♩. = 60-69)

Write the chord names.

Write the Roman numerals.

ped. simile(similarly)

rit.

8va

Grand Cadence in F

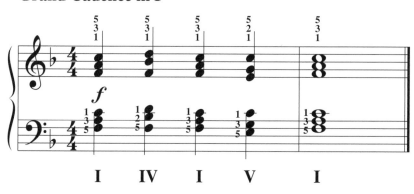

I   **IV**   **I**   **V**   **I**

MEMORIZE this cadence.

DISCOVERY

Play the Grand Cadence using an Alberti bass in the left hand. (R.H. plays blocked chords.)

Ex.   **I**

$\frac{6}{8}$ is often counted with 2 beats or PULSES per measure (instead of 6 beats per measure).

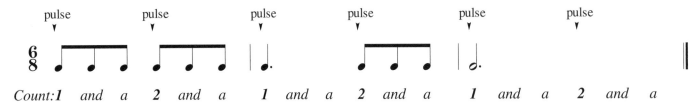

Count: *1* and *a* *2* and *a* *1* and *a* *2* and *a* *1* and *a* *2* and *a*

New Time Signature

$\frac{12}{8}$ is often counted with 4 beats or PULSES per measure. The ♩. gets the beat.

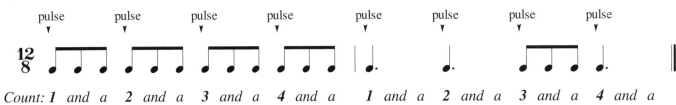

Count: *1* and *a* *2* and *a* *3* and *a* *4* and *a* *1* and *a* *2* and *a* *3* and *a* *4* and *a*

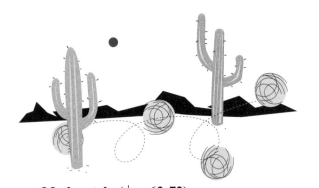

Tumbleweed Blues

N. Faber

Moderately (♩. = 63-72)

Count: 1   2   3   4   etc.

FF109

DISCOVERY Can you play the L.H. alone (with pedal) while your R.H. taps beats 1 - 2 - 3 - 4 in your lap?

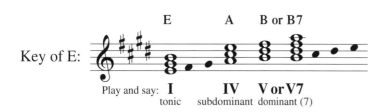

Key of E:

E   A B or B7

Play and say: **I**   **IV** **V or V7**
     tonic subdominant dominant (7)

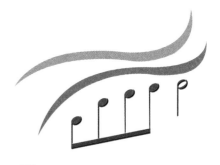

Rolling River Etude
(L.H. Accompaniment Study in E)

Write the
chord names.

Flowing (♩ = 104-116)

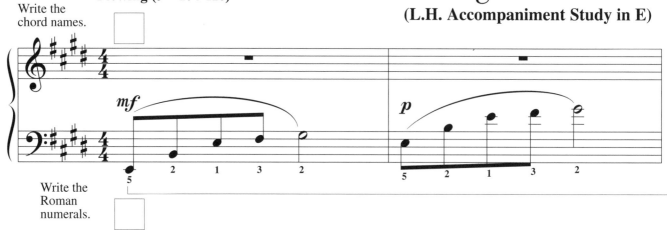

mf   *p*

Write the
Roman
numerals.

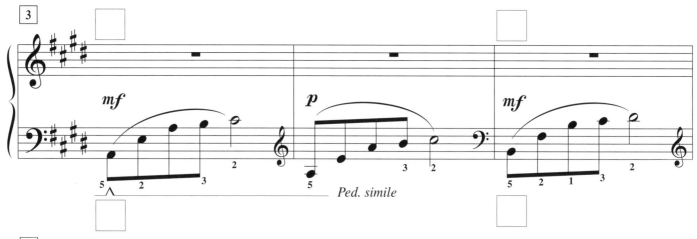

mf   *p*   *mf*

Ped. simile

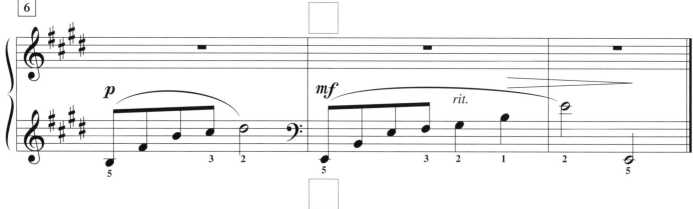

p   *mf*   *rit.*

Grand Cadence in E

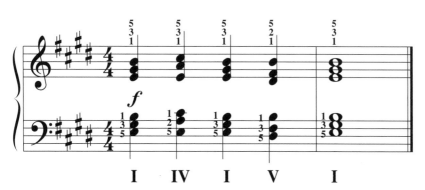

I **IV** **I** **V** **I**

MEMORIZE this cadence.

D I S C O V E R Y

Play the Grand Cadence 3
times, moving up an octave
for each repeat. Use pedal.

14

FF109

This American song is about the Shenandoah river which was named after the great Indian chief Shenandoah.

Play the right hand melody expressively, with a deep, rich tone. The accompaniment may remind you of the rolling river valley.

Finger Substitution

The R.H. silently changes fingers in *measure 7*.
Practice this finger substitution before playing the piece.

Shenandoah

American folk song

Gently rolling (♩ = 104-116)

Oh

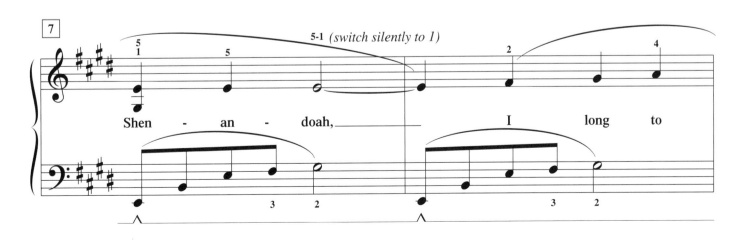

Shen - an - doah, _____ I long to

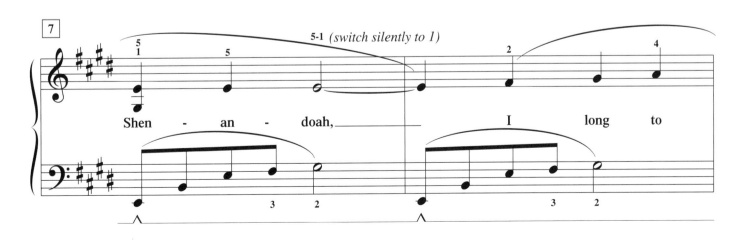

Theory p. 7

F1093

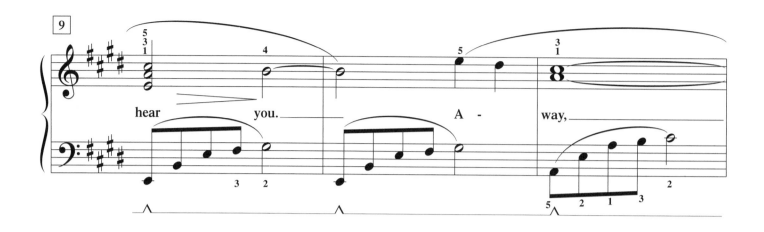

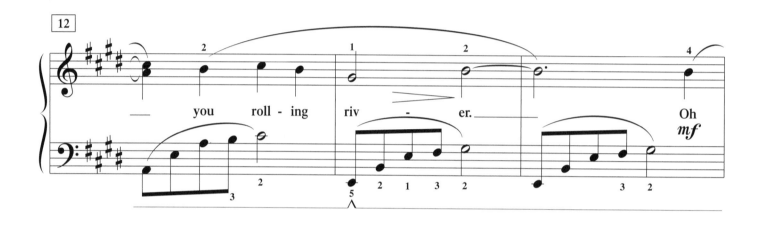

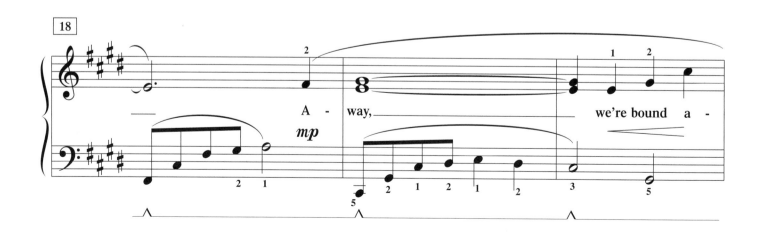

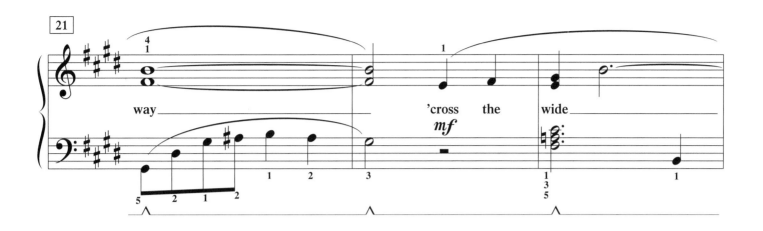

way_____ 'cross the wide_____

mf

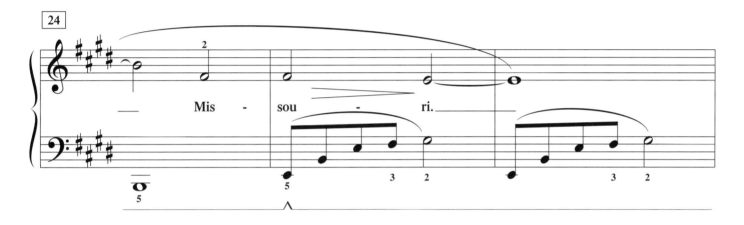

Mis - sou - ri.

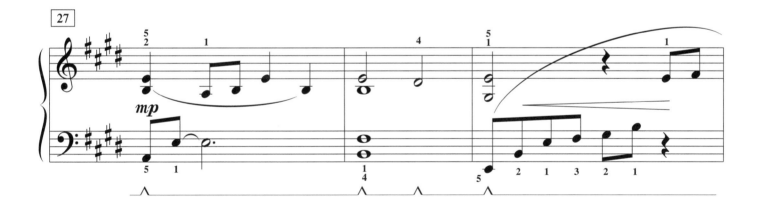

mp

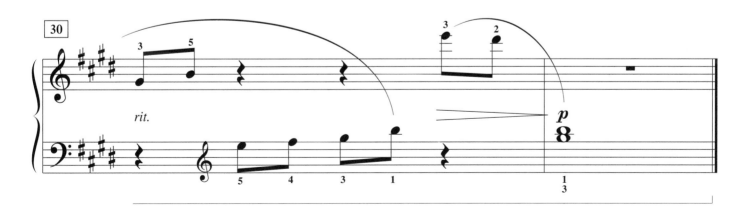

rit.

p

DISCOVERY Point out the final **V-I** cadence in the piece.

Naming Intervals

Perfect Intervals (4th, 5th, octave)

The intervals of a **4th, 5th,** and **octave** are called **perfect** intervals.
Perfect intervals are neither major nor minor.
(Use the letter "P" to label perfect intervals.)

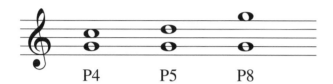

P4 P5 P8

Ear Training: Close your eyes and *listen*.
Practice naming the intervals as your teacher
plays perfect 4ths, perfect 5ths, and perfect octaves.

Major and Minor Intervals (2nd, 3rd, 6th, 7th)

The intervals of a **2nd, 3rd, 6th,** and **7th** can be either major or minor.
Study and play the examples below. (**M** = major; **m** = minor)

2nds

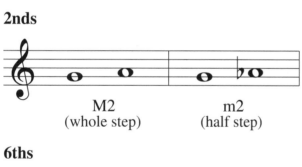

M2   m2
(whole step) (half step)

3rds

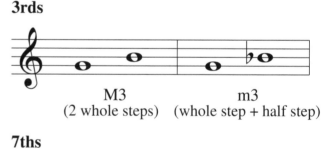

M3   m3
(2 whole steps) (whole step + half step)

6ths

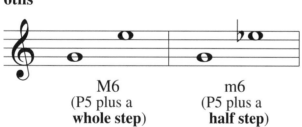

M6   m6
(P5 plus a (P5 plus a
whole step) **half step**)

7ths

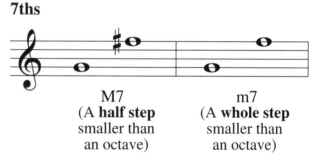

M7   m7
(A **half step** (A **whole step**
smaller than smaller than
an octave) an octave)

Interval Travel: Play these intervals on the piano. Can you land on the correct key?

Play C
- Up a P4, then
- Down a m7, then
- Up a M3

Did you land on B?

Play F
- Up a m3, then
- Down a P5, then
- Up a M7

Did you land on C?

Play D
- Up a m6, then
- Down a m2, then
- Up a m7

Did you land on G?

FF10

Practice Technique Review

1. Practice hands alone for **notes** and **rhythm.**

2. Play hands together S-L-O-W-L-Y for **articulation.**

3. Play at a moderate tempo for **dynamics.**
   Mark any difficult measures (X) for extra practice.

The Chase
Op. 100, No. 9

Name the intervals in the boxes on this page.

Hint: Include the **P** (Perfect), **M** (Major), or **m** (minor).

Johann Burgmüller
(1806-1874, Germany)
original form

cadence on
I or **V** *(circle)*

cadence on
I or **V** *(circle)*

agitato—means excited

Theory p. 12, 13, 14, 15, 16

*pronounced "do-LEN-tay"

rallentando—same as *ritardando*

DISCOVERY This piece represents an English fox hunt.

Which section of the piece suggests the fox's point of view?

The Circle of 5ths

The circle of 5ths will help you learn scales and key signatures.

- For flat keys, circle to the left, moving DOWN by perfect 5ths.

- For sharp keys, circle to the right, moving UP by perfect 5ths.

The next to the last flat is the name of the key.

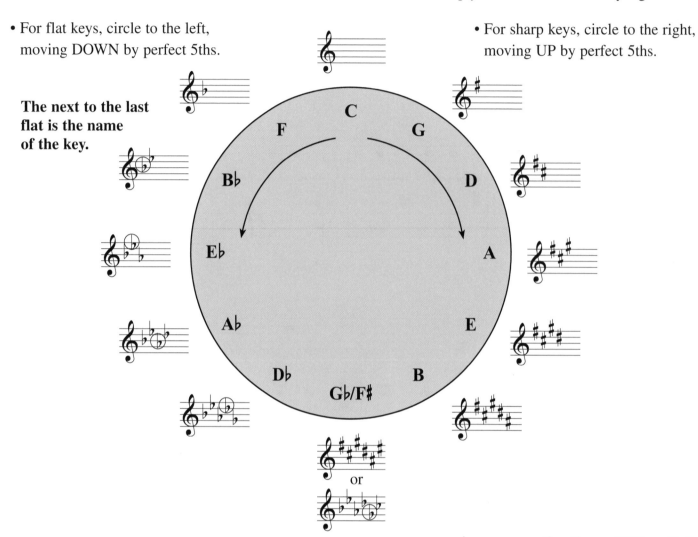

Around the World

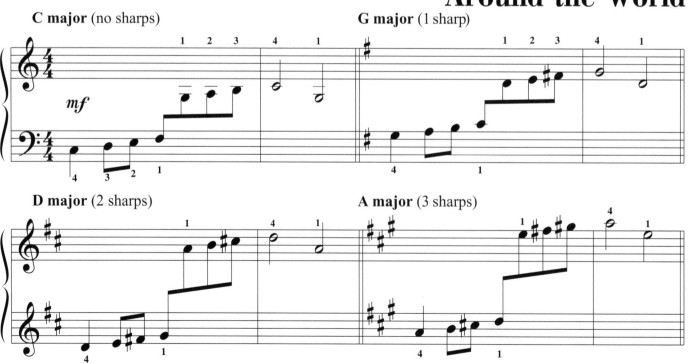

Note: For visual reinforcement, accidentals have been included along with the key signature.

FF109

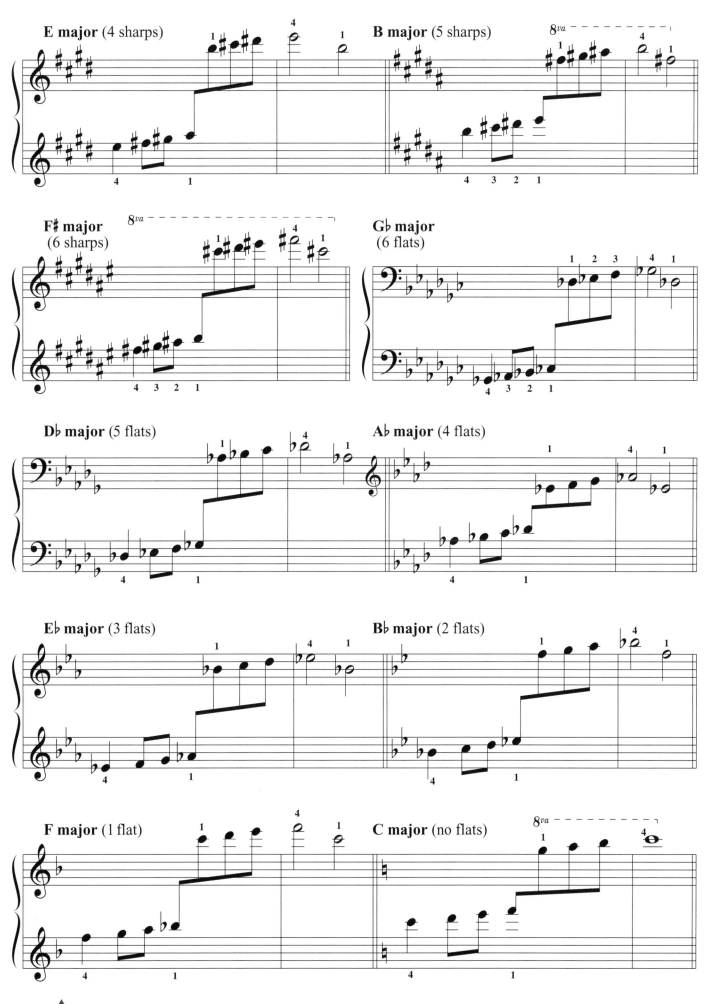

Can you make up your own exercise using the circle of 5ths?
Try using blocked or broken chords, one-octave arpeggios, or another musical pattern.

F1093

This lush, chordal piece follows the circle of 5ths moving counterclockwise (**down a 5th**).

The **roots** of the chords are named for measures 1-6. Write the roots of the chords for measures 7-16.

più mosso—means more motion (faster)
Circle this new term in your music.

Autumn Ballad

N. Faber

FF109

DISCOVERY

The form of this piece is **A B A** with a *codetta* (short ending). Label each section.

Two-Octave Arpeggios

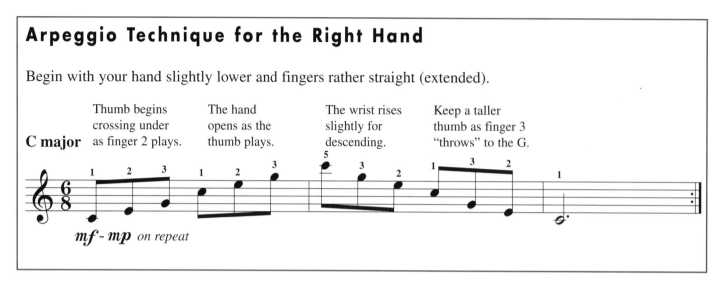

Arpeggio Technique for the Right Hand

Begin with your hand slightly lower and fingers rather straight (extended).

Thumb begins crossing under as finger 2 plays.

The hand opens as the thumb plays.

The wrist rises slightly for descending.

Keep a taller thumb as finger 3 "throws" to the G.

C major

mf - mp on repeat

G major

mf - mp

D major

mf - mp

A major

mf - mp

E major

mf - mp

B major

mf - mp

DISCOVERY

Can you play a 3-octave arpeggio for the right hand?

FF10

The student may proceed with the pieces that follow while learning these arpeggios.

Arpeggio Technique for the Left Hand

Begin with your hand open and fingers rather straight (extended).

Keep a taller thumb as finger 4 "throws" to the E.

The hand lowers slightly for the descent.

Thumb begins crossing under as finger 2 plays.

For a complete illustration of all the major 2-octave arpeggios, see
Achievement Skill Sheet #5, Two-Octave Major Scales & Arpeggios.

Practice Hint: Write an X above *measures 5* and *7*.
Give these measures extra practice as
you learn the piece!

Whirlwind
Op. 141, No. 14

Cornelius Gurlitt
(1820-1901, Germany)
original form

Allegro (♩ = 100-120)

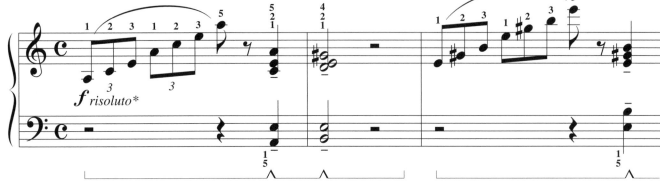

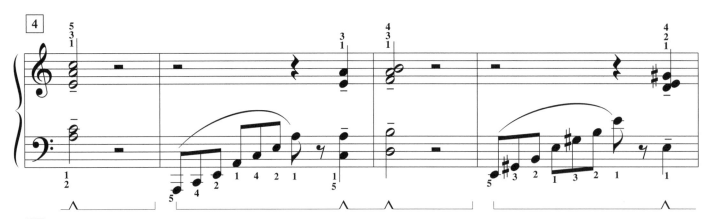

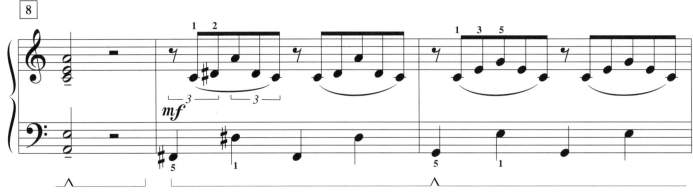

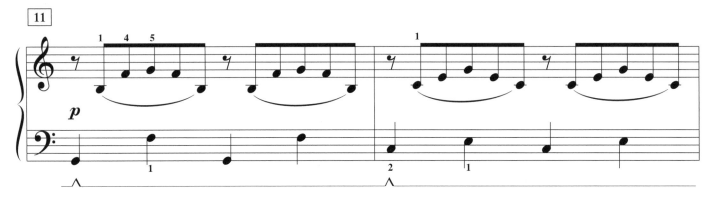

risoluto—means decisive

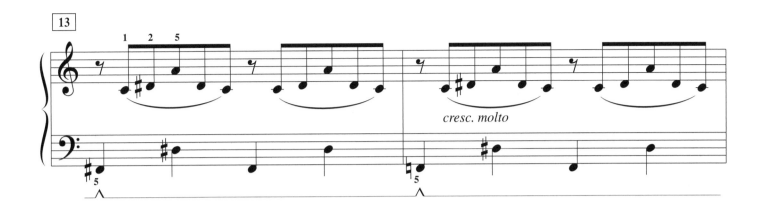

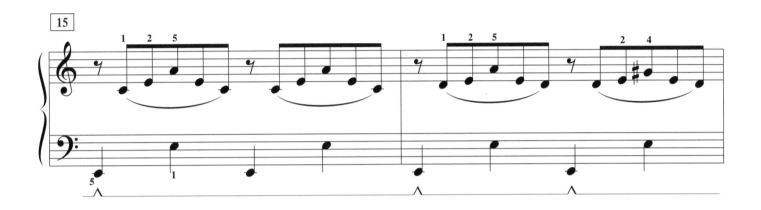

CREATIVE

Compose a short "Whirlwind" of your own using arpeggios for the right hand.

Use this chord progression: **Am - GM - FM - EM**

Hint for the left hand: Use triads, octaves, or a single note on the root.

St. Louis Blues is the most recorded popular song in history, with the exception of *Jingle Bells.* Enjoy learning this blues favorite!

Arpeggiated or Rolled Chord:

Play the notes quickly, bottom to top.
(Hint: Let your wrist rise in one smooth
motion as you play to the thumb.)

St. Louis Blues

W.C. Handy
(1873-1958, U.S.)
arranged

*Play the 8th notes in a long-short "swing rhythm."

30

DISCOVERY Write **I, IV,** or **V7** below *beat 1* of each measure on this page.

Flat Key Signatures

To name a key signature with flats, follow this rule:

The next to the last flat is the name of the key.

B♭ major   E♭ major   A♭ major   D♭ major   G♭ major

Circle the next to the last flat and name the key signatures below.

_____ major   _____ major   _____ major   _____ major   _____ major

The Flat Pattern

There are 7 flats in a complete pattern: **B♭ E♭ A♭ D♭ G♭ C♭ F♭**

1. Always begin with B♭.

2. Continue the pattern moving **up a 4th** and **down a 5th**.

Write a complete flat pattern daily for the next five days of your practice.

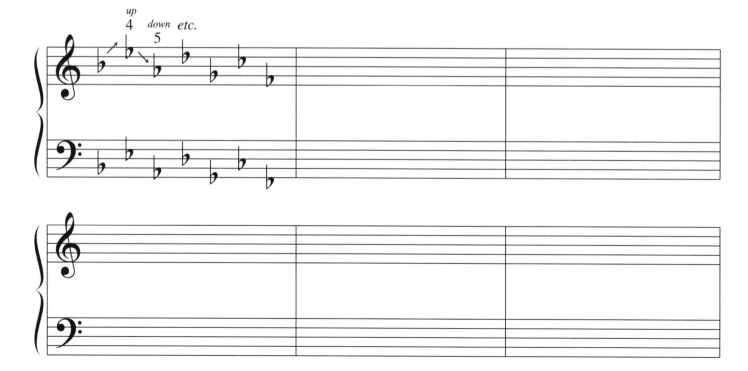

Theory p. 24-25

FF1093

The student may proceed with the pieces that follow while learning these flat scales.

Two-Octave Flat Scales

Play these scales hands separately before playing hands together.
Your teacher may set metronome goals and suggest dynamics.

Fingering Secret: For flat scales, the right-hand thumb always plays on C and F!*

F major

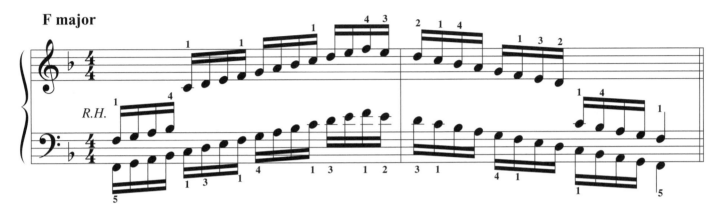

R.H. ♩ = ___   L.H. ♩ = ___   H.T. ♩ = ___

Use with p.34, *Risoluto*
p.36, *When the Sun Rises...*
p.38, *After You've Gone*

B♭ major

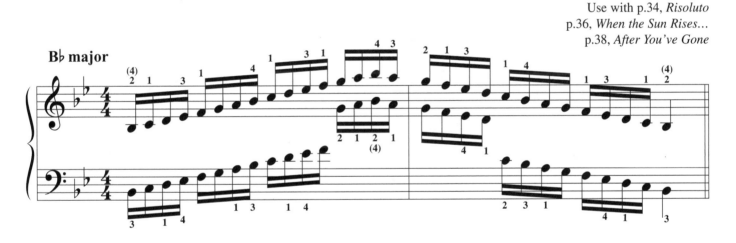

R.H. ♩ = ___   L.H. ♩ = ___   H.T. ♩ = ___

Use with p.40, *Pomp and Circumstance*
p.42, *Carillon Fantasia*

E♭ major

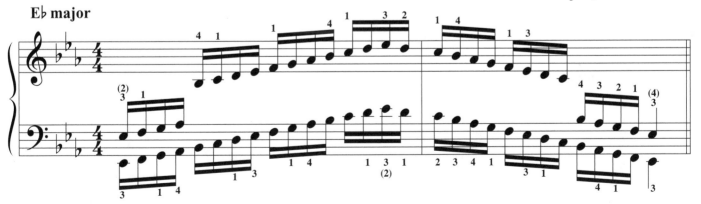

R.H. ♩ = ___   L.H. ♩ = ___   H.T. ♩ = ___

*In the G♭ scale the thumb plays C♭.

Theory p. 26, 27

FF1093

33

Grand Cadence in B♭

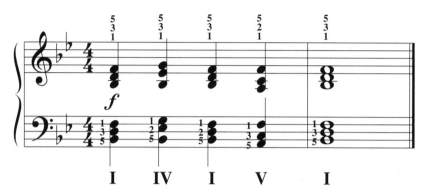

I   IV   I   V   I

Can you play the Grand Cadence in B♭ with the left hand
playing only the **root** of each chord?

I (tonic) = ____ **IV** (subdominant) = ____ **V** (dominant) = ____

Risoluto

Johann Christian Bach
(1735-1782, Germany)
original form

cadence on
I or **V**? (circle one)

FF1093

cadence on
I or **V**? *(circle one)*

cadence on
I or **V**? *(circle one)*

DISCOVERY Find and label two broken V7 chords (F7) for the left hand.

Sound Check:

Is your L.H. playing
softly while your R.H.
"sings" the melody?

When the Sun Rises...

N. Faber

cantabile—means singing (pronounced "con-TAH-bee-lay")

FF109

DISCOVERY Write **I, IV,** or **V** to show the harmony in measures 10-15.

This majestic arrangement of *America* features the big sound of L.H. octaves.
(If you can't reach an octave, play only the lower note.)

Fanfare on *America*

Samuel F. Smith

Slow March

FF1093

DISCOVERY The harmony of *measure 7* is in 1st inversion. (The 3rd is in the bass.)
What is the chord letter name?

Grand Cadence in E♭

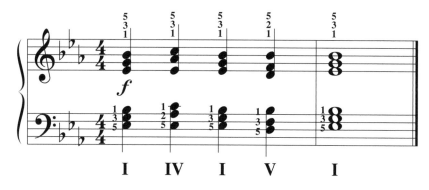

I   IV   I   V   I

Can you play the Grand Cadence in E♭ with the left hand playing only the **root** of each chord?

I (tonic) = ___   **IV** (subdominant) = ___   **V** (dominant) = ___

Pomp and Circumstance is one of five marches which Elgar composed for orchestra. The title is taken from a phrase in Shakespeare's play *Othello*. This ever-popular march has become a standard for high school and college graduations.

Pomp and Circumstance

Edward Elgar
(1857-1934, England)
arranged

Adagio (♩ = 66-80)

FF1093

Performance p. 20   Theory p. 30

DISCOVERY Point out a phrase which cadences on the V7 chord; a phrase which cadences on the I chord.

Think of this piece as having two different "planes" of sound:

- The accented notes should ring clearly and joyously.

- The broken-chord and scale passages should provide a contrasting "wash of sound."

Carillon Fantasia

R. Faber

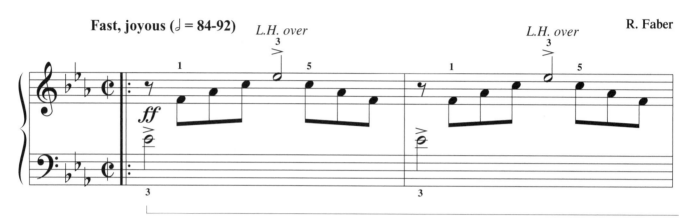

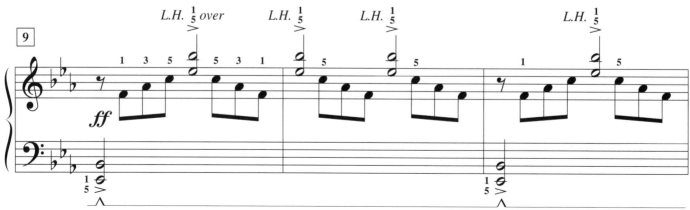

FF1093

DISCOVERY Point out two places where the musical ideas in *measures 1* and *2* are used later in the piece.

Review:

A key signature represents both a major key and a minor key.
The minor key *(relative minor)* is easily found by counting down
3 half steps from the tonic of the major key *(relative major)*.

Three Forms of Minor Scales

The **natural minor scale** uses only the notes of the key signature.

A natural minor scale

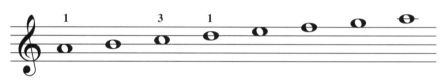

The **harmonic minor scale** is formed by *raising the 7th step* of the natural minor scale.

A harmonic minor scale

The **melodic minor scale** is formed by *raising steps 6 and 7* of the natural minor scale.

However, when the scale descends, the natural minor scale is used.

A melodic minor scale   *Natural minor when descending!*

Minor Scale Practice

Use with p.46, *Two Guitars*

R.H. ♩ = ____   L.H. ♩ = ____   H.T. ♩ = ____   (teacher chooses)

FF109

The student may proceed with the pieces that follow while learning these minor scales.

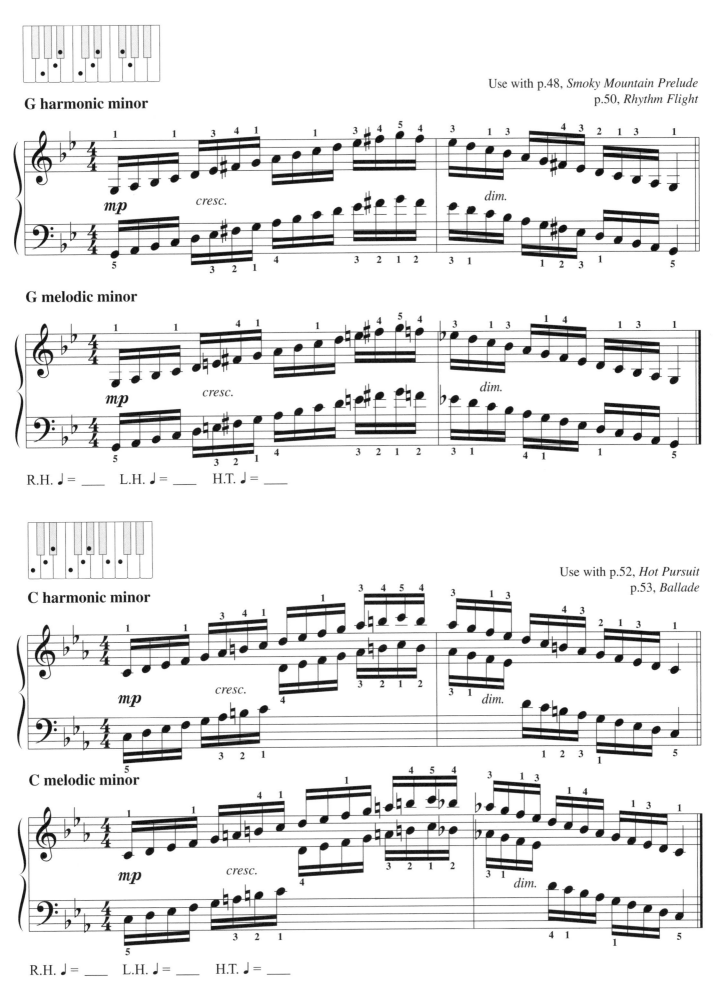

G harmonic minor

Use with p.48, *Smoky Mountain Prelude*
p.50, *Rhythm Flight*

G melodic minor

R.H. ♩ = ___   L.H. ♩ = ___   H.T. ♩ = ___

C harmonic minor

Use with p.52, *Hot Pursuit*
p.53, *Ballade*

C melodic minor

R.H. ♩ = ___   L.H. ♩ = ___   H.T. ♩ = ___

For a complete illustration of all the minor scales and arpeggios, see
Achievement Skill Sheet #6, Two-Octave Minor Scales & Arpeggios Booklet.

Primary Chords in Minor Keys

In a minor key, the **i** and **iv** chords are minor triads.
(Small Roman numerals indicate minor.)

The **V** chord uses an accidental to form a major triad.
(The accidental is from the harmonic minor scale.)

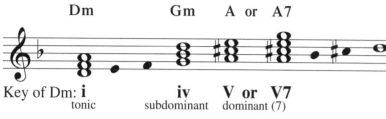

For a chord inversion exercise, transpose *Coral Reef Etude* (p.6) to D minor.

Two Guitars

Traditional

FF1093

Return to the **%** sign and play to *Fine.*

Improvise a short "snake charmer" melody:
Play a low L.H. 5th on D-A.
Use the notes of the D harmonic minor scale for the R.H. (Pedal as needed.)

Grand Cadence in Gm

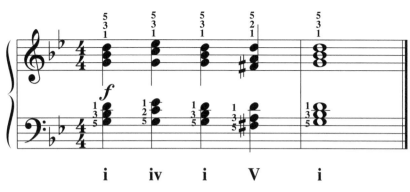

i   iv   i   V   i

Can you play the Grand Cadence in Gm with the left hand playing only the **root** of each chord?

i (tonic) = ___   **iv** (subdominant) = ___   **V** (dominant) = ___

Technique Hint: The italic text will help you keep a relaxed, flexible wrist.

Smoky Mountain Prelude

N. Faber

Moderato (♩ = 108-120)

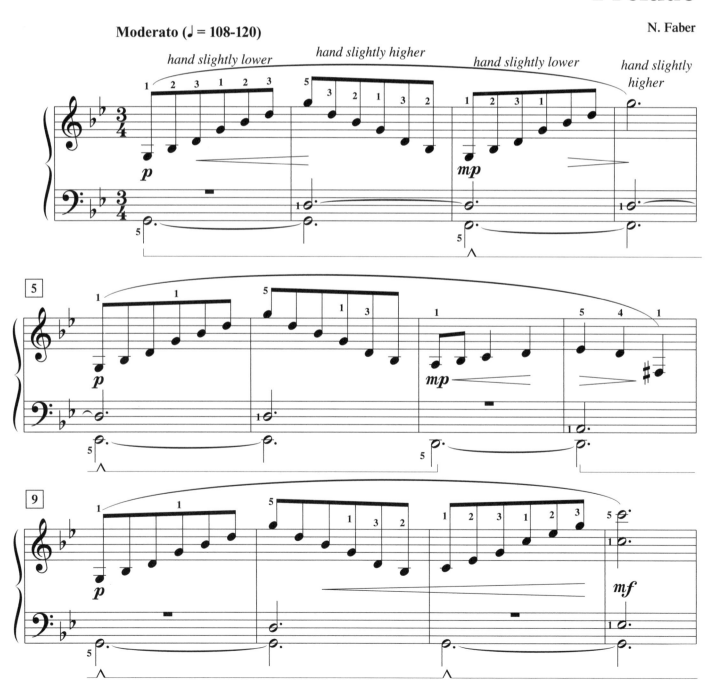

hand slightly lower   *hand slightly higher*   *hand slightly lower*   *hand slightly higher*

FF109

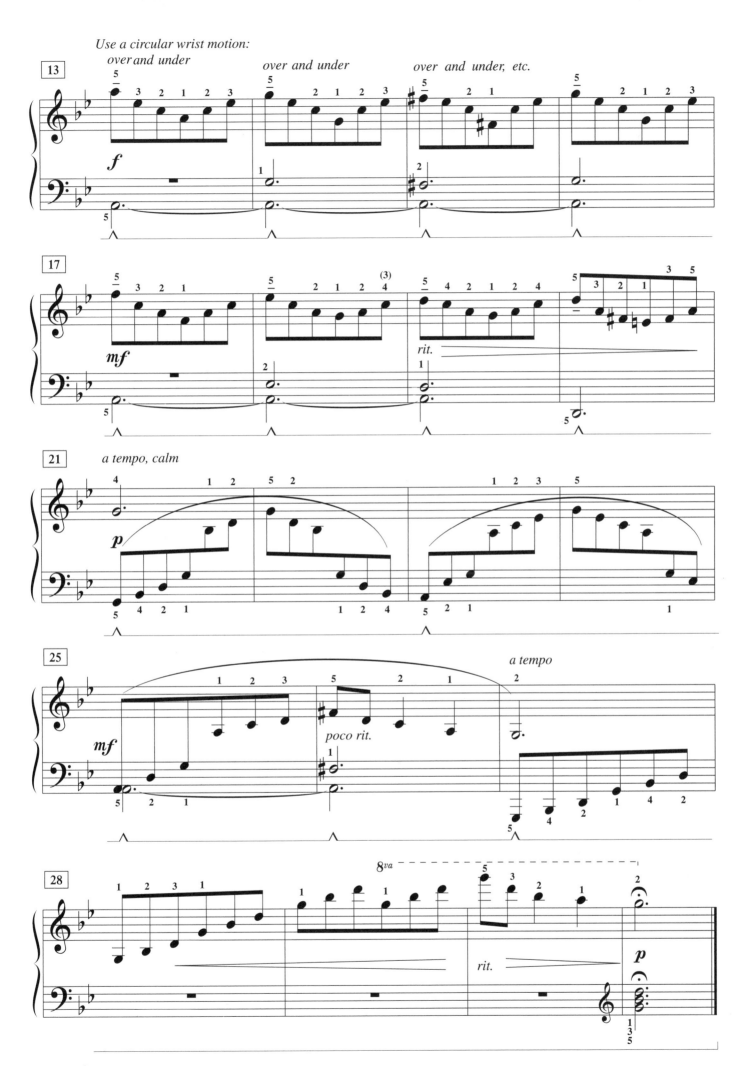

F1093

This piece uses **changing time signatures**.

To feel the pulse and rhythmic drive, count as shown.

Rhythm Warm-up: Tap and count the first page on your lap.

Be sure to tap with the correct hand!

Rhythm Flight

N. Faber

Energetic, driving

FF109

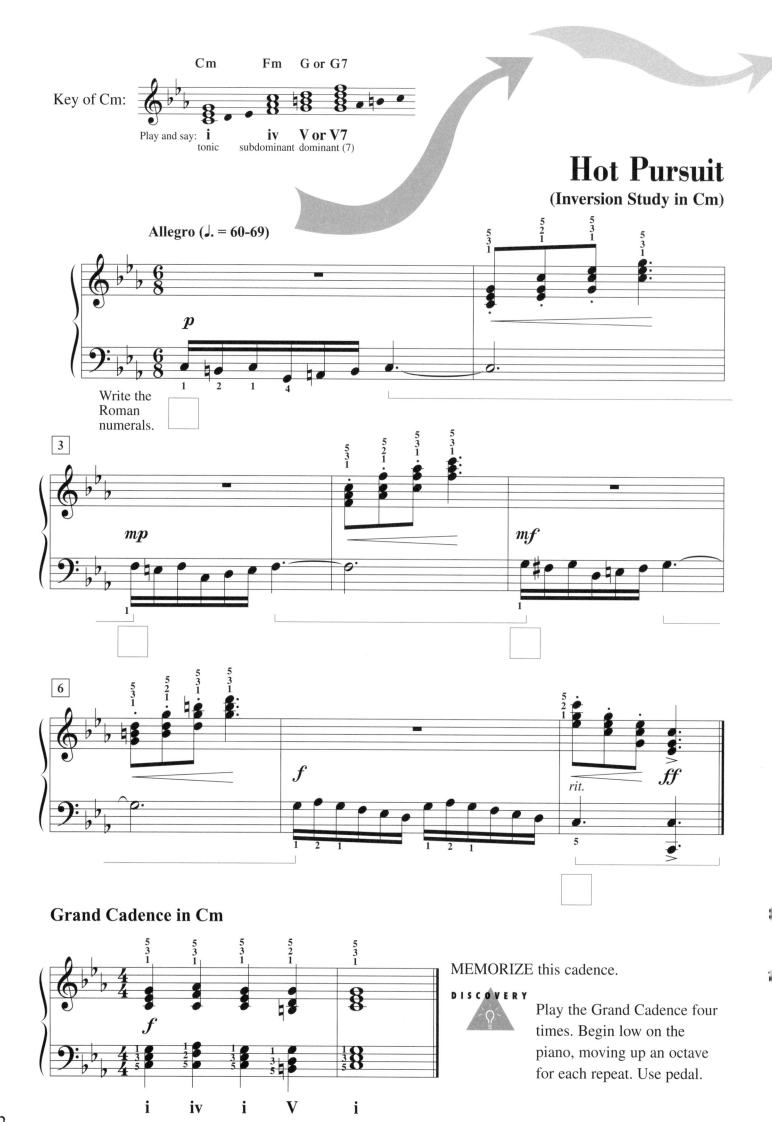

Key of Cm:

Cm   Fm   G or G7

Play and say: **i**   **iv**   **V or V7**
           tonic   subdominant   dominant (7)

Hot Pursuit
(Inversion Study in Cm)

Allegro (♩. = 60-69)

p

Write the Roman numerals.

3

mp   *mf*

6

f   *rit.*   *ff*

Grand Cadence in Cm

f

i   **iv**   **i**   **V**   **i**

MEMORIZE this cadence.

DISCOVERY

Play the Grand Cadence four times. Begin low on the piano, moving up an octave for each repeat. Use pedal.

FF109

Relative major and minor keys share the
same key signature. (Ex: CM and Am)

Parallel major and minor keys share the
same tonic. (Ex: CM and Cm)

Is the **B section** of this piece in the *relative* or *parallel* major key?

Ballade

Johann Burgmüller
(1806-1874, Germany)
original form

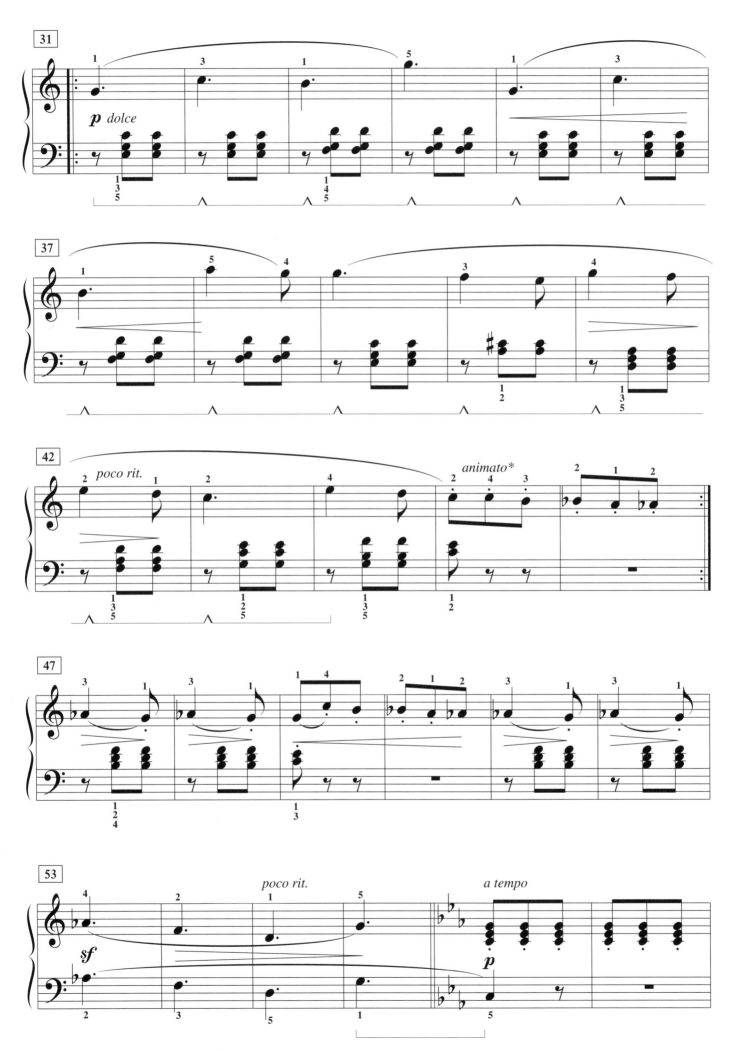

animato—means with spirit

Certificate
of Achievement

CONGRATULATIONS TO

_____

(Your name)

You have completed

Piano Adventures® Level 5

Teacher: _____

Date: _____